April '98

12⁵⁰

Cale,

Set your goals from your dreams, and turn them into your own reality.

Rick E.

Mini-Cooper & S

TIMO MAKINEN

PAUL EASTER

Mini-Cooper & S

COLOUR, DATA AND DETAIL ON
THE ROAD AND RALLY CARS
1960s TO 1990s

Nigel Edwards

GREENWICH EDITIONS

This edition published in 1997 by

GREENWICH EDITIONS
10 Blenheim Court
London N7 9NT

First published in Great Britain by

Windrow & Greene Ltd
5 Gerrard Street
London W1V 7LJ

A C.I.P. catalogue record of this book is available from the British Library.

ISBN 0 86288 180 3

Designed by:
ghk DESIGN, Bedford Park, Chiswick, London

Printed in China

Contents

Acknowledgements

Many enthusiastic people have been involved in the making of this book. As with my previous volume in the same series, this one has been a joint effort with Simon Painter, who provided most of the pictures.

Thanks are due to the owners of the various cars featured for having taken the time and trouble to bring their vehicles to the Quantocks, the Somerset Levels and the forest areas of the Mendip Hills where they were photographed.

Most of all, I would like to thank Dave Gilbert, proprietor of Classic Coopers of Burnham-on-Sea and Ex-Works Registrar of the Mini Cooper Register, who gave unstintingly of his time and energy, as well as his vast knowledge of all things Mini-Cooper and access to his unique collection of BMC Competition Department material.

I am also grateful to Leo Jacks, Gary Dickens and Steve Harris, for allowing me to draw freely on their enthusiasm and expertise; to Phillip Splett of the Mini Cooper Register for photographs and information; and to the various other photographers whose work is reproduced here.

Thanks to Gerda Kennedy and John Plummer, for their design and editorial work respectively; and to my wife Jean and daughter Charlotte for help and encouragement throughout.

Nigel Edwards
Wedmore, Somerset

Introduction

For those whose memories go back that far, mention of the Mini immediately evokes images of the swinging sixties: Jean Shrimpton and the mini-skirt, Carnaby Street and King's Road, pubs and boutiques with the obligatory Mini-Cooper S parked outside. The story of how Alec Issigonis conceived and designed the Mini, and how BMC launched it in 1959, has been told many times. Suffice it to say that almost three and a half decades later we still revere and cherish that amazing little car — and it is still in production, a record surpassed by very few other models indeed.

Concerning its sporting offshoot, the Cooper, two brief quotations sum up its appeal admirably. The first comes from *Motor* magazine and was penned shortly after the car's debut in September 1961:

This is the fastest production saloon car of its size ever to figure in our regular series of Road Test Reports. So much performance, combined with a lot of practical merit and quite a high standard of refinement, will obviously make many people decide that a sum of about £680 is better spent on this model than on something bigger but no better.

And this comes from *Classic and Sportscar*, more than three decades on:

Symbols of the sixties. We all recognise the car, but who's the suspicious-looking character alongside it?

Any Cooper, old or new, has the ability to put an ear-to-ear grin on your face. Forget the jittery ride, uncomfortable seats and noisy engine, and enjoy instead the chuckable handling and razor-sharp steering.

Above: *Mini-Cooper 997cc — a fine example of a car which is now hard to find in original condition.*

Below: *The 998cc engine gave no increase in power but was more robust and more driver-friendly.*

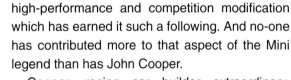

Not only in Britain but elsewhere in Europe, and especially in Japan, the Mini is still very much a cult car; in particular the Mini-Cooper and its even quicker stablemate, the S, are avidly sought and are cared for and driven by their owners with every bit as much pride — and often infinitely more pleasure — as cars of far greater financial value. Indeed, if one were asked to name a classic car which is the direct antithesis of the kind of hyped-up, ultra-expensive vehicles which are purchased not to be driven and enjoyed but simply for their perceived investment potential and/or value as status symbols, the Mini-Cooper would be the perfect candidate.

Besides the simple fact of its brilliant design in standard form, it is also the tremendous adaptability of the Mini and its aptness for high-performance and competition modification which has earned it such a following. And no-one has contributed more to that aspect of the Mini legend than has John Cooper.

Cooper, racing car builder extraordinary, Formula 1 World Champion Constructor in 1959 and 1960, and a good friend of Issigonis, was quickly convinced that the Mini was an ideal candidate for tuning. Meeting with little response from Issigonis, Cooper went to the then-boss of BMC, George Harriman, and obtained an initial agreement for just 1,000 Mini-Coopers to be produced — sufficient, in other words, for motor sport homologation. The Mini's 848cc engine was enlarged to 997cc and given twin carburettors to provide a substantial improvement in performance over the standard car. The result was an instant commercial success. Launched in July 1961, those earliest Coopers are nowadays rare and, if in original condition, correspondingly valuable.

Within less than two years, in March 1963, came a further step: because Formula Junior single seaters had an engine capacity limit of 1100cc, Cooper had instigated the development of a suitable racing version of the basic BMC A-series engine which the Mini shared with other small Austin and Morris models, and it was logical to de-tune it again for road use to take further advantage of the Mini's excellent handling. By now, Issigonis too was enthusiastic about the competition capabilities of his car — and BMC managers liked the publicity potential — and thus was born the 1071cc Mini-Cooper S.

With a further capacity increase, to 1275cc, the concept was developed right through to March 1970, when the Mk3 Mini-Cooper S arrived. But the end came in July 1971, as part of the rationalisation and cost-cutting exercises undertaken by a troubled British Leyland. It was the opening of a period which was to see the demise or emasculation of all the group's truly sporting models, with milestone cars like the MGB, Jaguar E-type and Triumph TR series following the Cooper S under the axe. Wherever enthusiasts gather,

Above: Mini-Cooper S — 1071cc (centre) and 970cc (right). It was with the introduction of the S that the Mini-Cooper really began to show its sporting possibilities.

Above, right: BMC introduced the Mini-Cooper 1275S in March 1964 and kept it in production for three-and-a-half years…

Right: … when it was replaced by the Mk2 version. Changes were mainly cosmetic, although the following year the all-syncromesh gearbox was introduced.

Above: *The Mk3 1275S arrived early in 1970 and, despite lasting for only fifteen months, is recognised as one of the most practicable and enjoyable of all Mini-Coopers.*

Below: *The Mini-Cooper reborn. Although contemporary refinements (and cost considerations) make it anything but a replica of the originals, it retains that all-important 'fun' element and has probably created even wider interest in its ancestors.*

the arguments over the necessity of such action will probably never be resolved, but what is clear with hindsight is that important market sectors were ceded to overseas manufacturers; hence, for example, the number of Japanese sports cars and coupés on Britain's roads today.

The Mini, though, survived in basic form and won new friends as time passed, which made it possible, in 1989, for a new Mini-Cooper to appear, something which would have seemed extremely improbable a decade earlier. One result has been an even greater interest in the original Mini-Coopers, now a focus of attention for those young enough not even to remember them. Fortunately, they are among the most affordable and practical classic cars available, still often less expensive than the modern article.

Those who have owned a Mini-Cooper will be fully aware of just how much interest and enthusiasm it can generate. Everyone either owned one once, or knows someone who did, or always wanted one. It is a car which positively inspires affection. There are other sought-after cars which look great but are brutes to drive; there are those which cost so much or are so difficult to repair that their owners hardly dare use them; and there are others with no real flair which are classics today and devalued tomorrow. The Mini-Cooper falls into none of these categories: it is immensely enjoyable to drive, its owners have a huge network of spares suppliers and specialist services to call on, usually at moderate cost, and it is a genuine milestone — a significant one, for all its diminutive size — in motoring history. Why ask for more?

Reinforcing the classic status of the little car is its impressive competition pedigree. It was fortuitous that the Mini-Cooper story began almost at the same time as the redoubtable and perceptive Stuart Turner took charge of the BMC Competition Department. The following year, 1962, witnessed Pat Moss and Ann Wisdom achieving seventh overall in the demanding Monte Carlo Rally. This was followed by a win in the Tulip Rally and subsequently, as the car grew in power and reliability, there came a succession of outstanding performances through the mid-1960s by such drivers as Makinen, Aaltonen, Hopkirk and others, which have become part of rallying legend.

In racing, though nowhere near as competitive at international level, the Mini-Coopers proved ideal for the clubman (as they did in rallying too) — inexpensive for those participating, and a great spectacle for the many onlookers.

How is the atmosphere of those days, and the special character and appeal of so charismatic a car as the Mini-Cooper, to be translated into mere words and pictures? It is, of course, a problem which can never be entirely resolved. Even the best of motoring books is but a poor substitute for the primary experiences of owning and driving, just as the very best of travel books cannot possibly convey all the heady sensations enjoyed at first hand when arriving in a strange country…

The approach in the pages which follow has been to focus upon a representative selection of individual Mini-Coopers, photographing them in detail and writing about both the cars and their owners — all of whom, it might be added, are dyed-in-the-wool enthusiasts. It is through these cars as they are today, together with a look back at some details of the work carried out by the BMC Competition Department, that we hope to convey something of what these famous high-performance Minis were — and are — all about.

Below: Mini-Coopers still figure prominently in a variety of sporting events. This one is pictured at Martini Corner, a challenging 45-degree hairpin just before the finish on Wiscombe Hill Climb. *(Brooke Photographic)*

Mini-Cooper 997cc

Powering the first Mini-Cooper was the first of what was to become, over the years, a whole range of engines developed from the original 848cc Mini unit, itself a variant on the lengthways-mounted A-series used in cars like the Morris 1000 and Austin-Healey Sprite. In this case, the increase in capacity was obtained by lengthening the stroke rather than enlarging the bore diameter. Although approximately 25,000 997cc Mini-Coopers were built, few remain in existence today. Apart from the fact that more than 30 years have elapsed since their introduction and a large proportion of them have fallen by the wayside, many others were upgraded (for want of a better word) by enthusiastic owners of the time. To find a truly original early model, like the one shown here, will be considerably more difficult than locating, say, a Mk2 or Mk3 Cooper S.

Restored to its original specification and maintained in immaculate condition, VTK 132 was first registered in November 1963 and has belonged to its present owner, Brian Davage, for the past 10 years. Its paintwork is Old English White with the characteristic black roof which has come to be thought of as the hallmark of the Mini-Cooper … which is not to say, of course, that every Mini with a black roof is a Cooper, or that every Mini-Cooper had a black roof! In fact, it is far from uncommon for cars offered as Mini-Coopers to be nothing more than standard Minis in disguise, nor is it unknown for a genuine Cooper to be masquerading as an S. An application to the British Motor Industry Heritage Trust is one means of establishing a Mini-Cooper's authenticity, though not an infallible one. Membership of the Mini Cooper Register is so strongly advisable as to be virtually essential. In addition to its many other benefits, the Register has produced a comprehensive Buyer's Guide, available to members only, which provides invaluable information on what to look for when inspecting a potential purchase, including a detailed *Caveat Emptor* section.

997cc Coopers wore either the Morris or, as in this instance, the Austin badge. The only exterior features distinguishing the cars from standard Mini-Minors, as they were then called. were the duotone colour scheme, the chromium-plated grille, the Austin or Morris Cooper badge on the bonnet, and the additional corner rails on the bumper. The car had front disc brakes to complement its increased performance and inherited the basic Mini's compact dimensions and sharp handling. It was aptly described by *Motor* magazine as 'A wolf-cub in sheep's clothing'.

Rear view was also largely unchanged from the basic Mini, though
bumper rails featured again and the bootlid carried the words
Austin Cooper but no heraldic badge. The small, neat light clusters
were standard, as was the single fuel filler — twin tanks were yet to
come.

The car's functional, uncluttered interior has red and grey
upholstery typical of the period. The remote-control gearchange
was a special Cooper feature, with a lever considerably shorter
than on the contemporary standard car. The centrally mounted
instrument binnacle has separate oil pressure and water tempe-
rature gauges beside the speedometer (later adopted for some de
luxe non-Cooper Minis). The heater visible under the dash rail was
listed as an optional extra, as on most BMC cars of the time. The
sliding side windows were simple, provided good ventilation and
permitted large storage bins in the doors.

The 997cc engine (pictured overleaf) developed 55bhp, making performance considerably more lively than that of the standard Mini-Minor or Austin Seven which could muster only 34bhp. Mini driving, however, is more about the ability of the little car to keep up high average speeds across country on give-and-take roads with its 'on rails' roadholding than about out-and-out performance in a straight line. The only non-standard item here is the Downton badge on the rocker cover: Downton Engineering was one of the foremost engine tuners of the period, BMC-approved and working on both road and competition cars. This particular car has not been modified, however, but has been conscientiously maintained as original.

MINI-COOPER 997cc

PRODUCTION PERIOD: September 1961 to December 1963.
Number produced: approximately 25,000.

BODYSHELL: Steel unitary construction 2-door 4-seat saloon with front and rear subframes.
As standard Mini except for grille and some trim details.

ENGINE: Type 9F. BMC A-series 4-cylinder in-line water-cooled, transversely mounted.
Iron block and cylinder head. Chain-driven camshaft, pushrod-operated overhead
valves. Bore and stroke 62.43mm x 81.28mm, capacity 997cc, compression ratio
9:1 (8.3:1 optional). Twin SU HS2 1.25in carburettors.
Power 55bhp at 6000rpm, torque 54lb/ft at 3600rpm.

TRANSMISSION: Transfer gears, 4-speed gearbox with unsynchronised first gear, integral final
drive. Front-wheel drive. Gear train beneath engine, shares common oil supply.

SUSPENSION: Front; transverse wishbones, lower tie-rods, rubber cone springs, telescopic
dampers. Rear; trailing arms, rubber cone springs, telescopic dampers.
Rack-and-pinion steering.

BRAKES, WHEELS, TYRES: 7in discs front, 7in drums rear. 10in diameter 3.5in wide steel wheels;
5.20 x 10 crossply tyres, Dunlop Gold Seal standard.

DIMENSIONS: Wheelbase 80in/2032mm. Front track 47.75in/1213mm.
Rear track 45.9in/1165mm. Length 120.25in/3054mm. Width 55.5in/1410mm.
Height 53in/1346mm. Kerb weight approximately 1400lb/635kg.

PERFORMANCE: 0 to 60mph 18 seconds. Maximum speed 85mph/137kph.
Typical fuel consumption 30 to 34mpg.

PRICE: £569 in 1963.

Mini-Cooper 998cc

A couple of years after the Mini-Cooper appeared came the second non-Cooper version of the Mini engine, the 998cc unit first seen in the Riley Elf and Wolseley Hornet but soon available in the ordinary Austin and Morris too. Despite the closely similar capacity, it had different dimensions from the 997cc Cooper power unit, with a shorter stroke, and it was an inherently more robust design in some important details such as the connecting rods. The obviously logical next step was to use it as the basis for the Cooper, tuned in much the same way as the 997cc engine with twin carburettors and raised compression ratio. Sure enough, the switch was announced for early 1964, the car remaining otherwise unchanged.

Although working in London, Roger Hill has spent much of his free time restoring his 998cc Mini-Cooper to its current superb condition at his parents' home in Somerset, which is where it was photographed. This car was built and despatched to Marshalsea Motors, Taunton, in November 1963. Its engine number is 9FA-SA H117, indicating that it was the 17th 998cc Cooper unit built. BMC had stopped 997cc engine production around September that year and started production of the 998cc in November. It seems that by November there were no more of the earlier units in stock, and consequently 998cc Mini-Coopers began to appear earlier than the planned changeover date of January 1964. 931 VYC is believed to be the oldest 998cc Cooper still in existence.

The only discernible difference between the rear of this car and that of the 997cc model illustrated earlier is that this is a Morris rather than an Austin Cooper, with the lettering on the bootlid smaller and slightly more formal in style. The bumper rails and other features are unchanged, and this was how the Cooper would continue to look until October 1967 when it adopted the Mk2 Mini bodyshell for the last two years of its production life.

Front end too is unchanged. The additional bumper rails were shared later with the Cooper S but would disappear with the advent of the Mk2 shell (and they often went missing from earlier cars too!). The simple, easily cleaned steel wheels were usually shod with Dunlop Gold Seal tyres on delivery. Development work by Dunlop had been one factor in making possible the original choice of the 10in diameter for the Mini's wheels.

MINI-COOPER 998cc

PRODUCTION PERIOD: Late 1963 (officially January 1964) to November 1969.
NUMBER PRODUCED: approximately 74,000.

As Mini-Cooper 997cc except:

BODYSHELL: From October 1967, Mk2 body with larger rear window and rear lamps, new front grille shape.

ENGINE: Type 9FA. Bore and stroke 64.588mm x 76.2mm, capacity 998cc, compression ratio 9:1 (7.8:1 optional). Power 55bhp at 5800rpm, torque 57lb/ft at 3000rpm.

TRANSMISSION: From September 1968, all-synchromesh gearbox.

SUSPENSION: From September 1964, Hydrolastic system with fluid interconnection between front and rear rubber springs, integral damping, rear tension springs.

TYRES: From March 1964, 145 x 10 radial-ply tyres, Dunlop SP41 standard.

PERFORMANCE: 0 to 60mph 16.8 seconds. Maximum speed 90mph/145kph. Typical fuel consumption 30 to 32mpg.

PRICE: £590 in 1965, £710 in 1969.

The plain but eminently practical interior, with central instrument binnacle and a relatively large plastic-covered steering wheel, was common to all Minis and more or less unchanged till the arrival of the Clubman models at the end of the decade. When acquired by its present owner, this car had been slightly modified for rallying but over the last five years it has been gradually returned to its original state.

The rear-seat accommodation in the Mini was surprisingly good for a car of such small outward dimensions, and the large glass area contributed to giving the whole interior a light, airy feel. It's easy to forget how claustrophobic the insides of most small cars were until the Mini changed everyone's ideas about design.

Switching to the 998cc engine gave no increase in maximum power, at 55bhp, though it was now delivered at 5800rpm, compared with 6000rpm for the 997cc unit. There was a gain in torque, though, making the car smoother, pleasanter and more tractable. *Autocar* found this new Mini-Cooper 'noticeably livelier than those we have driven previously' and stated roundly, 'It is an extremely practicable car for city and country alike, and we do not foresee any need for radical alterations in its design for many years to come'.

Mini-Cooper 1071S and 970S

The first Mini-Coopers were successful in their own right, brisk little cars whose perky, willing character endeared them to all who drove them. But they also served to indicate that further development of the theme was eminently possible: the Mini, originally conceived purely as basic and economical transport, had capabilities inherent in its design, particularly in the area of handling and roadholding, which were by no means exhausted yet. With the advent of the Mini-Cooper S, the little car really began to put on some muscle and show signs of serious competition potential.

The search for an early Cooper S or two to illustrate the model in these pages led to a man whose enthusiasm emphasises the appeal of these cars and whose commercial activities underline the international spread of that appeal. Leo Jacks has been in business in the Somerset town of Bridgwater since 1971: he began with caravans but subsequently moved on to Minis and has been dealing in them ever since. Early in the 1980s he attended the Beaulieu Autojumble with a Mini-Moke he had restored and sold it within minutes of arriving. The following year a second Moke was bought by an Irishman, the year after that a Moke and a Cooper S were purchased by a customer from Luxembourg, and at the next year's Auto jumble came the first sale of a Cooper S to a Japanese buyer.

From these beginnings has grown a thriving export business. The Mini, and in particular the Cooper and S, are greatly in demand in Japan, where space, especially in urban areas, is at a premium and small cars have long been socially acceptable. Most of Jacks' clients are wholesalers selling on to garages who in turn sell to the eventual customer, and the end price of the cars can reputedly be as high as £30,000. In greatest demand are the Mk1 and Mk2 1275 Cooper S.

The workshop is also a regular supplier of spares to a dealer in northern Germany who has a large two-storey warehouse packed with anything and everything for Minis to cater for thousands of enthusiasts in his country. Exporting to both Japan and Germany usually demands infinite attention to detail: colours, fittings and trim parts must all be exactly right, with any missing or substandard components substituted with genuine replacements.

First appearance of the Mini-Cooper S was with the 1071cc engine and it quickly began to make its mark. *Motor* magazine called it 'a car of delightful Jekyll and Hyde character, with astonishing performance… and truly formidable competition potential at a very modest price' (£695 in 1963). Seen here outside Leo Jacks' workshop, BYB 975B is a restored example dating from January 1964, destined for a German customer and finished in correct period colours of Tweed Grey and Old English White.

No, the S badge is not straight! It never was when the cars left the factory and any restorer aiming for complete authenticity should avoid the error of straightening it. Standard Mini equipment was a hinged number plate so that you could drive with the bootlid down to accommodate something bulky. For German customers, though, the plate has to be fully secured to meet legal requirements.

From the front, only the S above the badge distinguishes the car from its contemporary Mini-Cooper 998cc stablemate. New front hubs to carry larger brake discs pushed the wheels out and widened the track, though, and the rear drums had integral spacers to match.

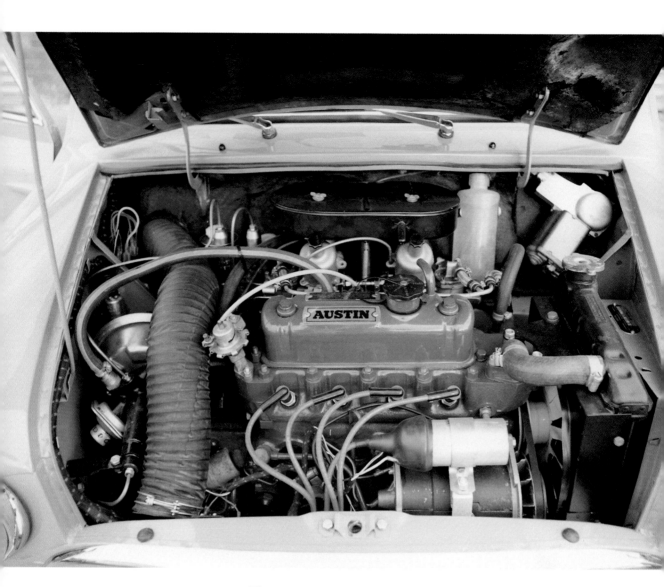

Though outwardly little changed, the new engine was extensively upgraded in detail. Sturdier and lighter connecting rods, a stiffer crankshaft, higher quality bearings, improved valve gear and a redesigned cylinder head all contributed to a significant power increase. But the car remained smooth and tractable: *Motor* commented, 'The Mini-Cooper S is an extremely fast car under any road conditions… although flexible enough at low speeds, the engine gets progressively happier as the revs rise.'

Replica Minilite-style wheels are the only non-standard items fitted to BYB 975B, at the customer's request. Though not as light and tough as the original genuine article, they do enhance the appearance. Standard wear was 3½ in-wide steel wheels, but the 4½ in alternative was a very frequently specified option.

MINI-COOPER S 1071cc
Further development of Mini-Cooper with short-stroke engine
based on Formula Junior racing unit.

PRODUCTION PERIOD:	March 1963 to August 1964.
NUMBER PRODUCED:	4017.

As Mini-Cooper 997cc except:

ENGINE:	Bore and stroke 70.6mm x 68.26mm, capacity 1071cc, compression ratio 9:1. Power 70bhp at 6000rpm, torque 62lb/ft at 4500rpm.
BRAKES, WHEELS, TYRES:	7.5in discs front, servo standard. 10in diameter steel wheels, 3.5in wide standard, 4.5in wide optional; 145 x 10 radial-ply tyres, Dunlop SP41 standard.
DIMENSIONS:	Front track 48.6in/1234mm. Rear track 47.3in/1201mm.
PERFORMANCE:	0 to 60mph 13.5 seconds. Maximum speed 95mph/152kph. Typical fuel consumption 27 to 30mpg.
PRICE:	£695 in 1963.

All restoration projects under-taken by Leo Jacks are carried through with commitment and care, and the car looks as good underneath as on top. The Dunlop SP tyres, with their di-stinctive tread, were *the* tyres of the era, used by BMC's Compe-titions Department, and are still available today. They provided excellent handling in both wet and dry, controllable, responsive and not prone to squeal.

In the boot, the cloth-covered wooden tray on which the tool roll is lying provides a flat load surface and can be pulled out to reveal the spare wheel neatly housed beneath.

31

The interior has received equally painstaking attention and nicely exemplifies the style of the period. Though externally small overall, the space-efficient Mini is surprisingly generous in its internal proportions, with adequate head room and rear seats which are much more habitable than the so-called 2+2 arrangement offered by many other sporty cars.

Unchanged for the Cooper S were the Mini doors with their sliding windows and those useful storage bins. Chrome scuff-plates and door handles reflect the prevailing preference for bright trim, in contrast to the 'no chrome' look of the 1990s. Here, the chromework is in first-class condition, but to remain so it will need regular cleaning and polishing.

The second Cooper S model to appear was the 970cc version. Leo Jacks has owned this example for six years and totally rebuilt it using the original engine but a new Mk1 bodyshell. Colour is the original Fiesta Yellow and the car has the Hydrolastic suspension introduced in September 1964, just three months before this car was registered. It retained rubber as the springing medium but

added hydraulic front-to-rear interconnection to reduce the choppy pitching movements characteristic of the Mini. Opinion was divided as to its success: ride comfort was generally improved, particularly for the leisurely driver, but lack of a self-levelling function gave the car a tail-down attitude when loaded, and rough surfaces and regular long-wave undulations could still prove uncomfortable. There are now aftermarket kits enabling adjustable shock absorbers to be added to control the bounce. Much later, Minis would revert to the 'dry' system.

The interior is trimmed in Surf Blue with silver brocade; it was probably trendy in its time but now has a somewhat dated appearance. Generally speaking, Mini-Coopers were not endowed with exciting colours, any more than were most other cars of the period.

MINI-COOPER S 970cc

'Homologation special' to qualify for under-1000cc class in international motor sport.

PRODUCTION PERIOD:	March 1964 to January 1965.
NUMBER PRODUCED:	972.

As Mini-Cooper 997cc except:

ENGINE:	Bore and stroke 70.6mm x 61.91mm, capacity 970cc, compression ratio 9.75:1. Power 65bhp at 6500rpm, torque 55lb/ft at 3500rpm.
SUSPENSION:	From September 1964, Hydrolastic system with fluid interconnection between front and rear rubber springs, integral damping, rear tension springs.
BRAKES, WHEELS, TYRES:	7.5in discs front, servo standard. 10in diameter steel wheels, 3.5in wide standard, 4.5in optional; 145 x 10 radial-ply tyres, Dunlop SP41 standard.
DIMENSIONS:	Front track 48.6in/1234mm. Rear track 47.3in/1201mm.
PERFORMANCE:	Maximum speed 92mph/148kph. Other figures not available.

The 970cc version of the S was available to special order only, being produced purely as a 'homologation special' to qualify the car for the under one-litre class in the international Group 2 Touring Car Championship. As soon as sufficient numbers had been built (by January 1965) production was halted, and the total was less than 1,000.

The distinctive drilled steel wheels first appeared on the 1071cc version and went on to become something of an S trade mark. Inevitably, the tuning shops enjoyed a lively trade selling them to be fitted to non-S Minis as well.

There never was a Cooper Traveller from the factory, (although one was shown by Cooper at the 1967 Racing Car Show), but perhaps there should have been! This one was prepared by Leo Jacks for his wife but, having been seen by a Japanese visitor, will quite likely find its way to Japan with orders following for more. It has the new Mini-Cooper engine, with twin carburettors, modified head and five-speed gearbox. Seats and interior are from a Mini Mayfair. Another kind of hybrid popular in Japan is the new Mini-Cooper saloon fitted with 1960s-style dashboard and oval instrument binnacle.

Mini-Cooper 1275S Mk1

The next step in the evolution of the Mini-Cooper S was the 1275cc version, introduced by BMC in March 1964. For a while, all three engine options, 1071cc, 970cc and 1275cc, were available to choice, but this situation was short-lived. With no 1100cc touring car class in international motor sport, there was no real *raison d'etre* for the 1071S; it was discontinued just five months later, and the 970S soon followed. The torquier 1275S was a much better bet for most purposes. In September 1964, *Motor* nominated it as 'Just about the most practical toy that £750 will buy'. To put that price in its contemporary perspective, a basic Mini was then £450, an MG Midget £625, and the larger Cortina GT was also £750. For performance, economy and the unquantifiable fun factor, the S was unbeatable.

The early cars were not entirely without their problems, however. Hard-driven examples tended to overheat. The Lockheed brake servo sometimes leaked (the pattern is no longer available and most owners fit the better Mk3 type). Pre-1968, there was no synchromesh on first gear, the second gear synchro was prone to wear, and the intermediate idler gears were often noisy. With time, though, all these things would be improved.

Superbly restored, FCV 694D is a September 1965 Mk1 1275S owned by Gary Dickens. Proprietor of Thornfalcon Garage, near Taunton, Somerset, Gary has been involved in cars all his life. His father's garage in the nearby town of Bridgwater took a BMC franchise in the mid-1960s; long before Gary was able to drive, he was spending hours in the show-room getting to know the cars, and particularly the Minis, inside out. His first car was a Mini and by the time he was 20 he had a 1071S. But it was not until 1977 that he obtained the example pictured here, and its condition was far from perfect. It had clearly reached the crossroads of its life and in the wrong hands would probably have ended up in the scrapyard. Fortunately, it fell into the right hands…

Gary's car is, by choice, not 100 percent original, but he has kept it uncomplicated and uncluttered by 'period additions'. The Webasto sunroof is a nice extra which does not spoil the lines: unlike most modern sunroofs, it opens the interior to a large area of sky.

MINI-COOPER S 1275cc Mk1

PRODUCTION PERIOD: March 1964 to October 1967.
NUMBER PRODUCED: approximately 14,000.

As Mini-Cooper 997cc except:

ENGINE: Bore and stroke 70.6mm x 81.33mm, capacity 1275cc, compression ratio 9.5:1. Power 76bhp at 5800rpm, torque 79lb/ft at 3000rpm.

SUSPENSION: From September 1964, Hydrolastic system with fluid interconnection between front and rear rubber springs, integral damping, rear tension springs.

BRAKES, WHEELS, TYRES: 7.5in discs front, servo standard. 10in diameter steel wheels, 3.5in wide standard, 4.5in wide optional; 145 x 10 radial-ply tyres, Dunlop SP41 standard.

DIMENSIONS: Front track 48.6in/1234mm. Rear track 47.3in/1201mm.

PERFORMANCE: 0 to 60mph 11.2 seconds. Maximum speed 96mph/154kph. Typical fuel consumption 27 to 29 mpg.

PRICE: £755 in 1964.

Brocade upholstery may seem a little eccentric to some, but it does give the car an added element of character. The interior is otherwise largely to original specification.

The Mini boot really is far from generous, especially when accommodating a tool kit and extra fuel. The second tank would have been a factory-fitted optional extra as it was not standard equipment until January 1966.

This is not one of those re-stored cars which are shielded from the elements. An avid hillclimber for many years, Gary is seen below in action at Wiscombe Park, in Devon. He has won several awards on 'the hill' — testament to his own driving abilities, the inbuilt strengths of the 1275S, and the skills of Steve Harris who prepares and maintains the car in his own workshop.

Steve Harris has been at the forefront of the Mini competition scene for three decades. He began an apprenticeship at Downton Engineering in 1964, aged 15, and worked his way through almost every department to end up as manager of 60 staff. Downton, founded and owned by Daniel Richmond, tuned MGBs, Austin Healeys and Mini-Coopers for the BMC works team and were recognised as pre-eminent in their field. Unhappily, the factory's interest in competition dwindled with the British Leyland takeover, and Downton finally closed in the mid-1970s. But Harris drew on the expertise he had gained and his close ties with Downton's former clientele to develop his own highly successful garage and tuning business. He is a first-rate driver too, winning the British Leyland 1275 Championship in 1979/80. Some 30 percent of his work is preparing cars for motor sport, 60 percent is restoration, and the remainder general servicing. Pictured above and overleaf is one of his charges, Jonathan Buncombe's beautiful Mini-Cooper S, prepared for historic rallying, a branch of the sport which has given the S a new lease of competition life. This car, which enjoyed a successful season in 1992, has a 1293cc engine producing over 100bhp.

7866 DF

Andrew Roland, an enthusiast for many years, stores his vehicles in a magnificent 'motor barn' near his house on the Somerset Levels. Among them are a Jaguar XK120, a 'Frogeye' Sprite, a Morris 8, an early Porsche 911 cabriolet… and an immaculate Mk1 1275S. AAM 447B is a very early car, dating from June 1964, and is therefore on 'dry' suspension. It is authentic right down to the see-through plastic seat covers — impractical in a heatwave but ideal for protecting the original upholstery. Seating was never the Mini's strongest point: as *Autosport* observed, 'the seats are uncomfortable, the backs being far too upright. We have become used to the "monkey on a stick" driving position of the Mini… (but) this superb high-performance version is worthy of more comfortable seating'. Original owners often fitted one or other of the reclining seats available on the accessory market, but the collector today tends to be more concerned with originality. Andrew has owned his car since 1981, and in 1985 Steve Harris rebuilt the engine to the Stage 3 specification developed by well-known Mini racer Richard Longman. The result is an S as quick as it is beautifully maintained.

46

Leo Jacks' Mk1 1275S, an early 1967 car, is completely standard in appearance, inside and out, except for the addition of genuine Minilite wheels, as used on the works team competition cars. By January 1966 the twin fuel tanks, previously an option, had become a standard S fitting, as had an oil cooler. Note the bare standard dashboard, emphasising the Cooper S' strictly functional approach to sporting motoring.

The 1275cc Cooper S engine was not as smooth or quiet as its smaller brethren, but it did offer a substantial increase in both power and torque, enough to produce very spirited performance by the standards of the day. It was tough enough to stand further tuning too; though outwardly unchanged, this example, like a good many, has been rebuilt and carefully improved, with lightened and balanced moving parts and a capacity increase to 1293cc.

Mini-Cooper 1275S Mk2

The Mini-Cooper S, along with the rest of the Mini range, progressed to Mk2 form in October 1967. Revisions for the Mk2 were mainly cosmetic: there was a new front grille shape, a larger rear window, larger rear lamps, some chrome trim around the door windows, a double-skinned bootlid and one or two minor interior changes. It was not until the following year that the Coopers gained the substantial advantage of the new all-

synchromesh gearbox. (Many competition cars, including the one pictured here, had the 'box further beefed up to take an increase in power.) Production of the Mk2 S continued until March 1970.

Nigel Edwards acquired this car, prepared for historic rallying, in November 1990, to add to his Porsche 911, MGB GT, Land-Rover and Frogeye Sprite. The vendor was Mike Rosum, who had very successfully completed the 1989 Pirelli Marathon in the car. It had then been registered EXF 217H, but later on, when AJB 144A came up for sale, Rosum snapped it up for its echo of the Monte-winning S of Makinen and Easter, AJB 44B.

Rosum consigned the car to highly regarded competition specialists Oselli Engineering to have the engine bored out to 1293cc and blueprinted. It is geared for high-speed work rather than out-and-out acceleration, though that could be altered with a change of final-drive ratio. The additional lamps are of the original Lucas pattern and hinge forward on their special brackets so that the quick-release grille can be removed for access to the engine. Leather retaining straps keep the bonnet shut at speed on rough terrain.

Minilite-style wheels are replicas (though they still don't come cheap!) and Mike Rosum fitted Yokohama tyres for the Pirelli Marathon. They proved excellent in the dry but failed to live up to expectations in the torrential rain encountered at Cortina, in Italy. While the latest Yokohamas are said to be much improved, the present owner is inclined to go back to the trusty Dunlop SP Sports which served the Mini-Coopers so well in the past.

AJB 144A has taken part in the Norwich Union RAC Classic Run for two years and it appears frequently at Wiscombe and other hill climbs. It is pictured below prior to the 1989 Pirelli Classic Marathon, while still owned by Mike Rosum, and (right) on the open road, as photographed by Dick Lankester, during the 1991 Haynes Classic Car Run, preceding a Frogeye Sprite and a Triumph Stag.

The replica works-style dashboard carries a Smiths stop-watch and Halda Speed Pilot — the latter essential for any sporting event and hard to find second-hand. This one was renovated by Halda in London and fitted by Dave Gilbert, of Classic Coopers in Burnham-on-Sea, who also maintains the car. Other true-to-period fittings include a Butler 'Bendi' map-reading light and a matt black Motolita steering wheel. Since acquiring the car, Nigel Edwards has also fitted the modern high-back rally seats used in most present-day motor sport events and required by the regulations in many cases. It would be nice, however, to replace them with period reclining and tilting seats which are now being reproduced. The obvious advantages of the high-back seats are offset by the fact that they cannot be tilted forward for access to the rear of the car, making it for all practical purposes a two-seater.

MINI-COOPER S 1275cc Mk2

PRODUCTION PERIOD: October 1967 to March 1970.
NUMBER PRODUCED: approximately 7000.

As Mini-Cooper S 1275cc Mk1 except:

BODYSHELL: Mk2 version of basic Mini body with larger rear window and rear lamps, new front grille shape.
TRANSMISSION: Mid-1968, all synchromesh gearbox phased in over several months.
PRICE: £921 in 1968.

Mini-Cooper S Mk3

By March 1970, when the Mk3 Mini-Cooper was introduced, the 998cc version had been out of production for almost six months, leaving the 1275cc S to carry the sporting banner alone. The Austin and Morris marque names had been dropped too, the cars being designated simply 'Mini' within the British Leyland range. But, nomenclature apart, little was altered for the Mk3. Wind-up windows and concealed door hinges (an apparent step forward which, ironically, complicated the rust problem), plus a few other minor refinements, brought the Cooper S into the seventies.

Despite a production life which lasted only until June 1971, the Mk3 was perhaps the S in its best and most practicable form. The example pictured here on the sands at Weston-super-Mare belongs to Andrew Brown and illustrates perfectly the effectiveness of Alec Issigonis' 'small car outside, big car inside' design. Andrew, who is well over six feet tall and 14 stone, likes nothing better than climbing easily into his Cooper S and using it as regular transport — though he has the choice of five cars including an MGB and a Triumph Stag.

Andrew has owned the car since 1990 and has had a considerable amount of work done on it. It has Spax adjustable shock absorbers, reversing lights as fitted to later Minis, two-speed wipers and Cibié halogen lights — all making for easier and safer driving. Overall, the car is now in superb condition. In 1991 it appeared in HTV's *Striking Sunday* programme celebrating the 30th anniversary of the Mini-Cooper.

MINI-COOPER S 1275cc Mk3

PRODUCTION PERIOD: March 1970 to July 1971.
NUMBER PRODUCED: approximately 19,500.

As Mini-Cooper S 1275cc Mk1 except:

BODYSHELL: Mk3 version of basic
Mini body with winding
windows and concealed
door hinges.
Badged BL and Mini
(Austin and Morris names
discontinued).
TRANSMISSION: All-synchromesh gearbox.

The engine bay of Andrew Brown's Mk3 S. Restoration work involved cutting away and replacing much of the front, and new wings have been fitted. During the production life of the 1275S power unit there were some detail revisions and improvements but no significant changes to the specification. Twin SU carburettors continued to supply the mixture to the end. A car like this is a delight to drive, capable of holding its own on cross-country roads against many of the current hot-hatch brigade. Bearing in mind prices which can be lower than that of a 1990s Mini-Cooper, and the ready availability of parts, this most practical of Coopers must surely be one of the best-value classics on the road.

The Factory Rally Cars

When they introduced the Mini-Cooper, and particularly the S, BMC did an incalculable service to club motor sport. In the years that followed, the cars were to appear in every form of local and national event for which they were eligible (and Mini-based specials stretched that definition well beyond what at first seemed likely) as more and more people discovered the adaptability of the design and the low cost of preparing the Mini for competition compared with most alternatives.

But it was successes in motor sport at the international level and, in particular, the achievements of the factory rally team, that really established the Mini as a legend in its own right. Giant-killing performances on tough major events like the Monte, the Tour de France, the Tulip and the RAC Rally put the car ineradicably in the history books.

Reasons for the success of the BMC works Cooper S in motor sport included the ideal characteristics of the vehicle itself, with its small size, excellent power-to-weight ratio and 'flingable' handling; the drivers, surely one of the most talented groups ever in a single team; and the dedication of the Competition Department, under the leadership of Stuart Turner, to the continued development and refinement of the cars. A good many items of equipment taken for granted in rallying today, and some which have been widely adopted for road cars too, first appeared at Abingdon in the 1960s.

Not surprisingly, the works cars, with their distinctive red and white colour scheme (normal production Coopers in red had black roofs), have become a focus of interest for enthusiasts. A few genuine examples have survived, and Dave Gilbert, a long-time student of the subject who runs Classic Coopers in Burnham-on-Sea and is Ex-Works Registrar of the Mini Cooper Register, has two in his care.

Pictured here at the start of the 1966 RAC Rally, GRX 310D was one of the most rallied of all the BMC Competition Department Minis. It appeared on most of the major events and was driven by many of the top drivers including Tony Fall, Timo Makinen and, on this event, Rauno Aaltonen partnered by Henry Liddon.

Present owner Dave Gilbert acquired the car in 1974. Its 1966 build-date told him it was a Mk1 although when bought, confusingly, it looked like a Mk2. Further research revealed that Tony Fall had damaged the car in 1967 and it was then stripped and rebuilt, retaining the basic Mk1 shell but with Mk2 appendages, for the 1968 Acropolis Rally. It was subsequently raced until 1970, but Dave decided to restore it to the 1968 specification in which it had started its last rally.

At full chat in the forest: Aaltonen and Liddon came through the 1966 RAC Rally virtually unscathed to finish fourth overall. It was on this event that Dave Gilbert, then a teenager among the spectators, first set eyes on the car he now owns. (LAT)

Dave Gilbert entered GRX in the highly competitive RAC Golden Fifty event, run in 1982 to commemorate 50 years of the RAC Rally. It is seen here on Prescott Hill Climb. Although this was the first time he had driven the car in anger and his first time up Prescott, Gilbert nevertheless achieved the fastest time on the first day of the rally.

The driver's side of the dashboard in GRX 310D presents
this formidable array of switch-
gear for the lights, electric
screenwashers, two-speed
wipers and so on — there's
even a cigar lighter, fitted at the
request of Timo Makinen! On
top of the dash, above the rev
counter, is a route-card holder:
directions for the simpler road
sections were sometimes put in
it to give the co-driver a chance
for a nap on the longer events.
The starter button, replacing
the standard key-start arrangement, is under the main
dashboard.

Prescott again: Gilbert and
GRX at Pardon Hairpin, the
driver hard at work and the co-
driver hanging on to the grab
handle. The silver strips in the
windscreen are the busbars for
the heating element: BMC
were early pioneers of this
equipment on the works Minis
and, while not all the drivers
liked it, it certainly had its uses
on snowy events like the Monte.

The navigator's side of the dashboard is well equipped too. The twin Heuer clocks — stopwatch on the left and eight-day clock on the right — are illuminated by four aircraft pea lights which have their own rheostat dimmer. To the right is the Halda twin distance recorder, accurate to one hundredth of a mile (wheelspin permitting!).

The co-driver also has a battery of switches in the door pocket with which he can operate the washers and wipers when the driver is otherwise occupied. All the additional electrical equipment on board necessitates no less than four fuse boxes.

The seating in these later works rally cars was very carefully designed and custom-built for the purpose. The driver's seat has little padding but a snugly shaped and very secure glass-fibre shell. The second seat has a headrest and can be fully reclined. This enabled the driver to sleep while the co-driver took the wheel — contemporary rallies mostly had far fewer overnight rest halts than has become common today.

The padded roll-bar extends above both seats and there is

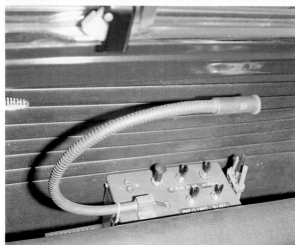

also padding down the B-pillars. The intercom system, now standard equipment for rallying, was something of an innovation when introduced by the BMC Comps Department in 1965. The matt black finish of the Motolita steering wheel, which helped to cut down unwanted reflections inside the car, was another new idea which has since become commonplace.

A complete distributor with leads attached and a set of fuel lines and hoses were among a welter of spares usually carried on rallies to enable the crew to keep going in the event of damage or breakdown in mid-stage. Visible in the boot here are the green FPT Industries fuel bag of the period, and a CO_2 cylinder with nozzles for inflating tyres, clearing blocked fuel lines or, in extreme cases, putting out fires.

The original-equipment Minilite wheels were made of magnesium alloy, stronger and lighter than the aluminium alloy more commonly used (including for the modern Minilite replicas) but unfortunately capable of becoming brittle with the passage of time. Modern tyres are fitted in place of the original CR65 racing tyres, used on tarmac stages, which would not be legal for road use today. The glassfibre wheel-arch extensions are screwed to the body and then neatly finished with the chrome trim moulding which was a standard S fitting. The 'Safety Fast' rosette emblem, borrowing an old MG slogan, was kept exclusively for works team use.

The most notable feature under the bonnet of GRX 310D is the use of twin split 45 DCOE Weber carburettors, an effective but very expensive ploy devised by the Competitions Department to take maximum advantage of the international regulations applicable in 1968. Cars were allowed to run with different carburettors from the standard specification provided the number of chokes remained the same, and these specially modified units conferred the performance advantage of the DCOE while staying within both the rules (though the French didn't think so!) and the limited space available in the Mini engine compartment.

On the road, GRX shows off the distinctive crouching silhouette of the well-set-up competition Cooper S, its poised, wheel-at-each-corner stance expressing something of the dynamic capabilities of this remarkable little vehicle. At low speeds, both clutch and steering seem heavy but, once the revs build up, the car is a driver's delight. For its owner, an outing in GRX is an infallible cure for the blues.

Rallying equipment developed by the works team in the light of experience included the front mud flaps which helped to keep the windscreen clean and protect it from self inflicted stone damage. The front lighting configuration had been changed after twin-filament halogen

Ex-works rally
MINI-COOPER S GRX 310D

Mk1 1275S extensively modified within limits set by international Group 2 regulations.

BODYSHELL:	Strengthened and with underbody protection.
ENGINE:	Capacity 1293cc, compression ratio 12.5:1. Downton-modified cylinder head, 649 camshaft, lightened steel flywheel. Twin split 45 DCOE Weber carburettors. Power output 100bhp+.
TRANSMISSION:	All-synchromesh close-ratio gearbox, straight-cut gears, limited-slip differential.
SUSPENSION:	Standard Hydrolastic with added anti-roll bar and heavy-duty bump stops.
BRAKES, WHEELS:	DS11 pads, VG95 rear linings, vented rear drums. 10in diameter 5.5in wide Minilite wheels.
PERFORMANCE:	'Adequate!'

bulbs became available, obviating the need to use two of the auxiliary lamps for dipped beam (the arrangement which had proved crucial in the notorious 1966 Monte Carlo Rally row when the organisers had excluded the Minis from first and second places after the event). Now, the two middle lights could be used as long-range driving lamps independent of the headlamps, leaving the outer pair of auxiliaries for use as fog lamps.

A powerful reversing lamp is fitted — but no rear window demister! The sump guard which protects the power unit has jacking points incorporated, though those on the bodyshell remain for use when the sump guard is removed.

The other ex-works car currently owned by Dave Gilbert, purchased by him in 1983, is seen here being driven by Paddy Hopkirk, accompanied by Henry Liddon, on the 1963 RAC Rally. Built for that event, with a 1071cc engine, 8 EMO was a very early Cooper S, production having begun in April the same year. In this, its first outing, it finished a highly creditable fourth overall. Hopkirk was a rising star then, his famous Monte Carlo win coming the following year. The location here is one of the sharp bends near the top of the Porlock Toll Road in Somerset, used as a special stage that year. Note the absence of both the driver's crash helmet, unthinkable on a special stage in later years, and a roll cage, which only became standard works rallying equipment after Hopkirk had a big accident on the 1966 Circuit of Ireland.

Shortly after the picture opposite was taken in BMC's Competition Department, 8 EMO (now with a 970cc engine) was shipped out to Minsk in Russia for the start of the 1965 Monte Carlo Rally in which it was to be crewed by Raymond Baxter and Jack Scott. A broken conrod unfortunately put it out of the event. It was one of just three cars that year running on the then-new Hydrolastic suspension. The skinny front tyres are fitted because the car has just come off the rolling road dynamometer. The fitment of a front grille muff reflects the icy conditions to be expected both in the start region and further south in the Alps in January. The seats have plastic over them to keep clean the cloth covering material, adopted for competition long before it became common on road cars. Visible in the back of the car are the twin washer bottles, moved inside to stop them freezing.

Interior shot of the restored 8 EMO reveals that, while some works cars had a full-width dashboard, the central instrument pod was retained in this case. An added panel on the driver's side brought the switches and rev counter closer to hand, while one on the co-driver's side carried the Halda Twin Master distance recorder which the team began to use early in 1965. Missing in this photo, unfortunately, is a Smiths eight-day clock, originally mounted to the left of the Halda. An early Simon Green steering wheel, of large diameter with a thin rim, was chosen for these 1965 cars. Also part of the 1965 Monte Carlo specification was the heated windscreen, and on this car the two halves can be switched on independently. The fuse box was below the dashboard on the nearside, and a fire extinguisher was mounted in the foot well (though not required by the regulations at the period).

The two seats, a deep bucket to hold the driver in place and a higher backed, fully reclining one for the co-driver, were both off-the-shelf items from Restall, used by clubmen and works teams alike. Microcell seats were tried too: custom-built seating for the factory teams came later.

The engine bay of any Cooper S was pretty full, and the works team cars at this period still looked more or less standard under the bonnet, the all-important tuning details being internal and hence invisible. Twin SUs still provide the carburation. The rally cars, with the hefty current requirements of all those lights, were early users of alternators instead of the old dynamo.

In this earlier version of the works team lighting configuration, five auxiliary lamps in two different sizes adorn the front end. Notice the straps to retain the headlamps. Evident too are the quick-release grille buttons and a substantial leather strap to keep the bonnet shut. Wheelarch extensions had not yet become *de rigueur* at this stage, though the tyres are barely contained by the standard wing shape.

From the rear, 8 EMO looks relatively innocuous and could almost be taken for a shopping car — an illusion rapidly dispelled by driving it, though! Until thoroughly warm, it is really a bit of a handful. A single Austin Healey 3000 sidelight serves as a reversing light.

Back in its natural habitat, on a Forestry Commission track, 8 EMO revives memories of past glories, tail hanging out, little tyres scrabbling for grip and sending up a barrage of flying gravel. Those who have heard it will surely not forget the sound of a rallying Cooper S in full cry, the howl of the gears intermittently drowned out by the fusillade of stones and rocks on the underside. At the end of a major forest event, the condition of the sump guard and floor bore witness to the fact that this was part car, part toboggan!

Ex-works rally MINI-COOPER S 8 EMO

Earlier version of the factory rally car,
less developed than GRX 310D.

ENGINE:	Capacity 1293cc, compression ratio 11.4:1. 510 camshaft, lightened steel flywheel. Twin SU HS4 1.5in carburettors.
TRANSMISSION:	Close-ratio straight-cut gearbox with unsynchronised first gear.
SUSPENSION:	Heavy-duty bump stops.

Close-up of one of the works team cars for the 1964 Monte Carlo Rally shows the headlamp washing system devised to try to keep the lamp clear of mud and frozen slush. There were two separate systems, one for the windscreen and one for the lamps, with the reservoirs inside the car, and they used an alcohol mix to inhibit freezing. Twenty years were to elapse before road cars began to get headlamp washers as standard equipment.

277 EBL ran in the 1964 Monte Carlo Rally but was completely burnt out following an accident. Fortunately the crew, Pauline Mayman and Valerie Domleo, escaped with only minor injuries. Details include an early windscreen heater, confined to the driver's side to limit current consumption. (One contemporary co-driver gave a hair-raising account of watching the snow banks advance and recede at speed on a Monte stage through the side window, the only place he could see out!) The heating element, developed by Triplex, comprised a very fine gold film on one of the inner faces of the laminated glass. Other fittings more typical of the period include the roof-mounted swivelling spotlamp, which could be directed by a handle inside the car to pick out signposts and markers, and the Monza quick-release fuel filler cap. The tyres are Dunlop SP44 Weathermasters, regarded as the ultra-grip tyres of the era and often used with studs fitted. The cars carried two spares in the boot and often two on the back seat as well.

Brand-new MGBs and Austin Healey 3000s, both models assembled at Abingdon where the Competitions Department was located, form a mouth-watering backdrop to this line-up of cars for the 1964 Alpine Rally. BMC continued to rally the big Healey alongside the Mini for some time, though it was ultimately the smaller car which gained the more noteworthy international success. AJB 44B, to the left of the Healey, went on to win the 1965 Monte in Makinen's hands. AJB 55B, extreme left, has an aluminium bonnet with two stiffening ribs, a design unique to this particular car.

Tony Fall doing his best to destroy CRX 91D during a test session. A lot of the underbody protection and suspension strengthening modifications which helped the works cars to their rallying successes were developed in rigorous testing of this kind. Details like bonnet and boot straps and mud flaps were proven this way too.

The boot of 277 EBL, clearly showing the two fuel tanks with their quick-release fillers. The protective boards attached to the inside faces of the tanks were adopted after a tank had been punctured by an unsecured studded spare tyre. The well worn tyres in this shot can be seen to have shed some of their studs.

This is the immaculate engine compartment of the works car
intended for Paddy Hopkirk to drive on the 1967 RAC Rally.
Foot-and-mouth disease led to the cancellation of the rally that
year, and this car went on to run in the 1968 Circuit of Ireland
where it broke its differential. Built to the prevailing Group 6
regulations, it used a single 45 DCOE Weber carburettor for the
first time. Interesting details include the studs on the wings for
headlamp stoneguard straps and the use of matt black wiper arms,
commonplace today but innovative when everything was bright
chrome. This engine has 'Morris' on the rocker cover, but the
choice of Morris or Austin identities was fairly flexible, depending on
publicity requirements, and some cars changed make from one
event to the next.

Inevitably best-known for its rallying exploits at all levels, the Mini-Cooper has featured consistently, and entertainingly, in numerous other forms of motorsport; including, as shown in these pictures by Peter Noad, in autocross and autotests. Pictured above are the 998cc Mini-Coopers of Lynden Downs and Judy Glading competing in an autocross at Shottesbrooke Park in 1968.

David Angel's Cooper S (above) in action at an auto-cross organised by Salisbury and Shaftesbury Motor Club in 1971.

Micki Vandervell (right) raising the dust and going absolutely sideways in her 998cc Mini-Cooper at the 1971 BTRDA Autocross Championship final.

Ken Irwin(left) was a regular member of the victorious Northern Ireland team in autotests, driving a 1275 Cooper S. Here he is seen competing at Ayr, Scotland, in 1972.

George Holland, seen below taking a very tight line around a marker cone in an autotest at Wallasey in his 1293 Cooper S in 1970, won the British National and regional championships in autotests.

John Larkin in Cooper S (right) smoking his tyres as he spins round a marker in an autotest at Huddersfield in 1973. Larkin was a regular and very successful competitor in the BTRDA Championships.

The New Mini-Cooper

The Mini-Cooper S was discontinued in 1971. As time went by, a new generation of sporty road cars, the hot hatchbacks, claimed the attention of enthusiasts and created a new market in which the major manufacturers battled for a share. In rallying, new names and a new era of rising speeds, escalating costs and increasing technical complexity changed the whole aspect of the sport. By all reasonable standards, it should have been the end of the Cooper story.

But the basic Mini was a survivor. Through all the vicissitudes of its parent company, the mergers and takeovers of the Leyland era, nationalisation and then privatisation again, the little car continued in production; it may have been eclipsed by later developments but it was never quite extinguished. Into the late 1980s, under the Rover banner, the Austin and Morris names long gone, it found renewed popularity as a series of cleverly packaged special editions caught the public eye. It might no longer be a major player in the small-car league, but the Mini was still there.

So, too, was John Cooper, no longer running a racing team but still in the motor trade and as enthusiastic as ever. He it was, in 1989, amid the celebrations of 30 years of Mini manufacture, who launched a new Cooper version, sold with Rover's blessing.

After something like twenty years and several changes of ownership, the old tooling had long gone, of course, and economic realities precluded its replacement, so that anyone looking for a close replica of the old car would be disappointed. But that was hardly the point. For many people, the much improved and updated details of the basic Mini (more comfortable seats, better soundproofing, proper fresh-air ventilation, instruments mounted in front of the driver, and so on) combined with cosmetic additions in providing a stylish and fashionably nostalgic reminder of its sporting past to make up a package which is just the job, and the new Cooper has sold well.

The example shown on the following pages belongs to Mike Gillings, local Mini-Cooper Register Secretary, and it's his 17th Mini — some kind of record?

Basically unchanged in 30 years of production, the Mini has survived to establish itself as one of motoring's great success stories. The duotone colour scheme of the new Mini-Cooper looks as good as it always did on the earlier models. Mike Gillings' October 1991 car has an accessory pack of spot lights, bonnet stripes and load tray in the boot. This was marketed under the title *Italian Job*, recalling the spoof thriller film in which the Mini's starring role effortlessly upstaged the human players. The bonnet stripes, though, are in the style adopted by the factory racing cars of the early 1960s which were run under the Cooper rather than the BMC banner: fact and fiction happily combine in the mythology of the Mini.

Under the bonnet, the A-type power unit soldiers on, with some detail refinements inherited from the later years of both Mini and Metro production, and the typically crowded appearance of the engine compartment remains. Note the special Cooper-inscribed ducting. This one has a catalytic convertor and so must use unleaded fuel, which has necessitated a change in cylinder-head specification as well as resulting in a slight power loss. Mike Gillings' is one of the last Coopers to be built with a carburettor: subsequent models have a single-point fuel-injection system. In the summer of 1991 the Cooper S title was revived, applied to a Rover-approved aftermarket conversion which pushes up power from the Cooper's 61bhp to a useful 78bhp at 6,000rpm. Outdated in many ways, by the standards of the 1990s, the Mini yet survives, and deservedly so, because it is responsive and fun to drive in a manner not remotely equalled by anything of comparable price. As ever, adding the Cooper dimension only enhances those qualities.

The style of the replica Minilite wheels is totally in keeping with the character of the car and, like the green and white colour scheme, echoes the Cooper's past sporting glories. Originally, though, the rims would only have been of ten-inch diameter, not 12, and low-profile tyres were unheard of in the 1960s. The laurel-encircled Mini-Cooper emblem is a nice touch.

The interior is largely the same as that of other current-production Minis, with many modern conveniences which suit today's new-car buyer very well, leaving the restorers and classic enthusiasts to cherish their more spartan original models. It's a great tribute to the inherent 'rightness' of the basic Mini design that it should have survived to be reborn in this way.

THE NEW MINI-COOPER

Current production Mini, basic design unchanged but with many detail refinements, plus added Cooper pack.

BODYSHELL:	6-year anti-corrosion warranty.
ENGINE:	Initially 998cc, twin carburettor, 64bhp.
	Then 1275cc, single carburettor, 61bhp.
	Subsequently 1275cc, single-point fuel injection, 63bhp. S option, 78bhp.
	Breakerless electronic ignition.
TRANSMISSION:	All-synchromesh 4-speed gearbox.
	Higher final drive gearing than earlier cars.
SUSPENSION:	'Dry' rubber cone springs.
BRAKES, WHEELS, TYRES:	Disc front, drum rear, servo assisted.
	12in diameter alloy wheels.
	145/70 x 12 low-profile radial-ply tyres.
PRICE:	£6995 in 1993.

Enthusiasm... The Mini Cooper Register

Mention has already been made in this book of the almost unique enthusiasm aroused by the Mini-Cooper, and nowhere is that enthusiasm more evident than in the Mini Cooper Register (without the hyphen), formed in 1986 and embracing the entire range through to the latest examples rolling off the line at Longbridge. John Cooper is the Register's Honorary President, while among its list of Honorary Members are Paddy Hopkirk, Paul Easter, John Handley, John Rhodes and others. In collaboration with Rover, the MCR hosted the 1989 International Mini Meeting at Silverstone, and in turn assisted Rover with the Mini 30 celebrations at the same venue.

The Register's monthly magazine is of an unusually high standard among club publications, twice winning a *Classic Cars* award, and regular monthly meetings are held in over 20 regions. Ownership of a Mini-Cooper is not a prerequisite for membership.

Shown below and at top of opposite page is the collection of cars owned by Phillip Splett, Chairman of the Register, at his farm in Barling, Essex, and his Mk1 998cc Mini-Cooper, at Bruntingthorpe.

Pride of ownership is reflected in this gleaming line-up of cars taking part in a concours during a Register gathering at 'The Manor' in Castle Coombe, home of the famous racing circuit.

Underbonnet views reveal the similarities between a well-maintained Mk3 S (right) and its Italian cousin, the Innocenti 1300, much less familiar in Britain but an interesting example of the sporting Minis' appeal to enthusiasts worldwide.

Above: Mk1 Cooper S is seen here at Prescott Hill Climb during the 1993 Norwich Union Classic Run, its green and white colour scheme echoing the exploits of the works racing team in bygone days.

Left: At any Mini Cooper Register event, the presence of one of the rare and cherished ex-works rally cars will always be a major point of interest.

Below, Left: Pictured here in the New Forest and reminding us that the Mini-Cooper is still very much alive and well, this 1.3 fuel-injected version has seen service as a factory demonstrator car.

Opposite: Reminding us that the Mini-Cooper did indeed see service as a police vehicle in some areas, this car featured in the MCR's 'Aspects of Mini Life' display at the Bromley Pageant of Motoring

Nigel Edwards *began his writing career in 1972 with a regular motoring column for his employer's international quarterly magazine. This led to requests for other articles from local publications and to talks on car testing at motor clubs and business dinners. He is a member of both the Institute of Advanced Motorists and the exclusive High Performance Club. He is also the author of the first book in the Classics in Colour series, on the Porsche 924 & 944.*

Among the vehicles he owns are a Porsche 911 T Lux, a totally original 1968 MGB GT, a 1972 Land-Rover, a 25,000-mile 1959 Frogeye Sprite, a 1965 Royal Enfield GT Continental motorcycle, and the Historic Rallies Mini-Cooper S featured in this book. Nigel Edwards lives with his wife and daughter, and among a very wide variety of animals, in a Somerset farmhouse.